Harriet Tubman and the Freedom Train

written by
Sharon Gayle

illustrated by
Felicia Marshall

Aladdin

New York London Toronto Sydney Singapore

To my husband, Oral, and my children, Nicholas and Rachael
—S. G.

To my husband, Brian, and son, Elijah
—F. M.

First Aladdin edition January 2003

ALADDIN PAPERBACKS
An imprint of Simon & Schuster Children's Publishing Division
1230 Avenue of the Americas
New York, NY 10020

Designed by Lisa Vega
The text of this book was set in Century Old Style.

Manufactured in the United States of America
10

Library of Congress Cataloging-in-Publication Data

Gayle, Sharon.
Harriet Tubman and the freedom train / by Sharon Gayle ; illustrated by
Felicia Marshall.— 1st Aladdin Paperbacks ed.
p. cm. — (Ready-to-read)
Summary: Introduces Harriet Tubman, from her birth into slavery, through her daring escape to freedom in the north, to her tireless efforts during the Civil War to free other slaves via the Underground Railroad.
ISBN-13: 978-0-689-85480-4 (pbk.) — ISBN-13: 978-0-689-85481-1 (library edition)
ISBN-10: 0-689-85480-3 (pbk.) — ISBN-10: 0-689-85481-1 (library edition)
0110 LAK
1. Tubman, Harriet, 1820?-1913—Juvenile literature. 2. Underground railroad—Juvenile literature. 3. Slaves—UnitedStates—Biography—Juvenile literature.
4. African American women—Biography—Juvenile literature.
[1. Tubman, Harriet, 1820?-1913. 2. Slaves. 3. African Americans—Biography.
4. Women—Biography. 5. Underground railroad.] I. Title. II. Series.
E444.T82 G39 2003
973.7'115—dc21

2002010042

Harriet Tubman
and the Freedom Train

Chapter 1
Born into Slavery

"I'll meet you in the morning,
When I reach the promised land;
On the other side of Jordan
For I'm bound for the promised land."

Harriet Tubman often sang when she was lonely or scared. This time Harriet was not scared. Harriet was free!

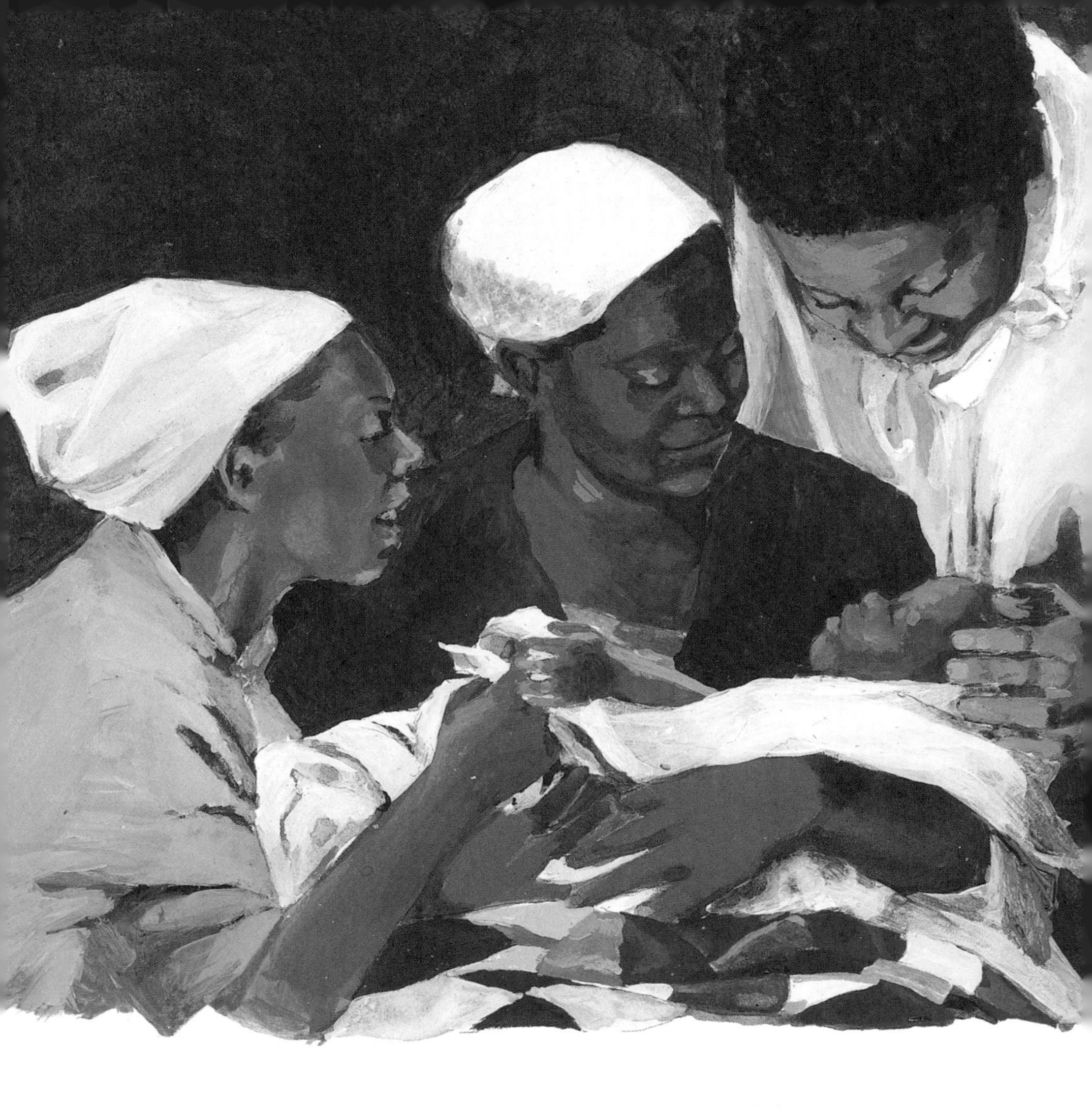

Harriet was not born free. She was born a slave. Her parents and brothers and sisters belonged to someone else. And so she did too. But her parents loved her. They decided to call her Araminta, or Minty for short.

They did not know that one day she would call herself Harriet. The night Minty was born, friends of the family came to visit. They were proud of the baby, but they wished all of them were free.

The life of a slave was very hard. Even small children had to work.

When Minty was still a young child she had to leave home and work for another family. At night she had to take care of their baby. In the daytime she had to help clean the house.

Minty's new owner was very mean. One day she tried to beat her. Minty decided to run away.

Minty quickly slid under the fence of the pigpen. She stayed there until night fell. When the pigs were fed, Minty ate some of their food.

After four days Minty was found. She was beaten so badly she had to go back to her mother.

As Minty grew older she went to work in the fields. Field slaves were treated very badly. They were often beaten with chains and leather straps.

Minty hated to see any living thing being hurt. She could not stand to see a helpless slave being beaten. But what could she do about it? She was only thirteen.

One day as Minty worked, someone shouted, “Runaway!”

Minty followed the slave and the slave owner. Soon the owner caught the slave and held him. He asked Minty to help him tie up the slave. Minty refused. The owner was so angry he threw an iron bar that hit her on her head. Minty was never the same.

Chapter 2
ESCAPE!

The injury hurt Minty very badly. She lay asleep for months. Finally one day in the spring Minty woke up. Her family was very happy. But Minty still was not well. She had horrible headaches. Sometimes she would fall into a deep sleep.

As Minty grew stronger, she went back to work. Her headaches and "sleeping sickness" did not keep her from becoming the hardest worker in the fields.

Outdoors Minty discovered secret hiding places. She even learned how to find food. Minty did not tell anyone about the hiding places or the food. She was sure that one day these things would keep her alive.

Soon Minty was getting married! John Tubman was handsome. Best of all he was a free man. But Minty's happiness turned to sadness: Marrying John Tubman would not make her free.

Worst of all John Tubman did not want her to be free. "If you try to run away," he told her, "I'll tell the master on you." Right then Minty decided she was going north no matter what.

Minty waited. By luck a white woman who lived nearby became Minty's friend. She told Minty, "Whenever you need help, you come and see me."

While John Tubman slept, Minty crept through the woods to the white woman's farm. The woman was glad to see Minty. She wrote two names on slips of paper and told Minty these were the people she should see next. Harriet was soon to learn that these were the next stops on the Underground Railroad.

Minty had heard of this railroad but she was surprised to learn it was not really a railroad at all. The woman explained that it was a group of people and places to stop for slaves who escaped to the North.

Minty left her friend's house with fear in her heart. She did not know if people were already looking for her. All she knew was that she had to keep moving north.

Minty only traveled at night. Each morning she would make her way to another stop on the railroad. There she would get food to eat and sometimes a place to sleep. Sometimes she had to work so that she would look like one of the slaves of the people who helped her.

Minty traveled every way possible. She traveled by foot, horseback, and wagon. Soon she found herself in Pennsylvania. She was free!

The first thing she did was look at her hands to see if she looked different. She was just the same, only free.

"From now on my name is Harriet," she said quietly to herself. "It's what I want to call myself now that I am free!"

Chapter 3
REWARD!

Once Harriet was free she found a job to take care of herself. Then she spent all her free time learning more about the Underground Railroad.

Harriet heard many stories of slaves who were trying to escape and needed someone to guide them to the North.

Suddenly Harriet knew what she had to do. She would return to the South. She wanted to help as many slaves escape as possible. She wanted all slaves to be free.

Harriet's most daring escape was with eleven people. Harriet had never guided so large a group before.

As the group traveled, they could hear the bloodhounds barking behind them. As the dogs came nearer, Harriet searched for a place to hide. But where was a place large enough to hold all of them?

Suddenly Harriet spied a huge pile of garbage. They jumped in the tower of garbage. Everyone breathed through straws and pipes. Soon the dogs lost the scent of the runaways. At daybreak the runaways went to a stream. They cleaned up and rested so they could travel that night.

After that Harriet Tubman became a legend. She made over fifteen trips back to Maryland to rescue slaves. She was able to rescue many of her brothers and sisters.

She was most proud of getting her parents to the North. She bought them a home in Auburn, New York. It was the first home her parents ever owned.

But Southern slave owners were very angry. They were mad that Harriet was taking their property away from them. The slave owners got together and offered a $40,000 reward for anyone who could bring in Harriet dead or alive. But no one ever found Harriet.

Now that a reward was being offered for Harriet, she had to be more careful.

Everywhere she went people were looking for her.

One time she was traveling on a train. She heard the bounty hunters storming through. She quickly picked up a newspaper, but she did not know how to read! Was she holding the paper right side up?

The bounty hunters had reached Harriet's car. She held her breath. They looked at everyone very carefully.

Suddenly she heard one of the men say, "No, that's not her. The one we're looking for can't read."

Harriet slowly let out her breath as the men kept going through the train cars.

Chapter 4
Spy and Hero

In 1861 a war broke out between the North and South. They were fighting each other over the right to own slaves. It became too dangerous for Harriet to guide runaway slaves to the North.

But Harriet did not let the war stop her from helping people. No one knew the woods and rivers in the South like Harriet. So she became a spy for the army of the North which was called the Union Army. In 1863 Harriet led a Union officer and black soldiers behind enemy lines. They rescued several hundred slaves and learned many of the South's war secrets.

Although Harriet helped many people find freedom, she remained poor. But she was proud. She was proud of her people. She knew many slaves fought amazing fear to escape their terrible lives.

Harriet was surprised how many people were proud of her, even people from other countries. She received a medal and letter from the queen of England to honor all the work she had done.

When Harriet died in 1913, her country showed they were proud of her. Harriet was buried with full military honors.

Here is a timeline of Harriet Tubman's life:

c.1820	Born as Araminta Ross in Maryland
1833	At age twelve or thirteen, receives a blow to the head that caused fainting spells for rest of her life
1844	Marries freeman John Tubman
1849	Escapes to Pennsylvania and changes name to Harriet
1851	Returns to the South and helped eleven slaves escape
1857	Rescues parents and brings them to New York
1860	Makes last trip to free slaves. She had made more than fifteen trips and rescued more than three hundred slaves
1861	Becomes spy for Union troops during the Civil War
1866	John Tubman dies
1868	Harriet's life story published
1869	Marries Civil War veteran Nelson Davis
1897	Queen Victoria honors Harriet with the silver medal and sends her a letter
1913	Dies in Auburn, New York, buried with full military honors